FREEING YOUR PASTOR TO SERVE WITH JOY
CEO or Homemaker: A Pastor's Heart Revealed

Rev. Jack S. Flietstra

FREEING YOUR PASTOR TO SERVE WITH JOY

FOREWORD

It brings me great joy when I hear of a pastor who has been at a particular church for a long time. Many pastors leave their ministries after just a short stay, which I believe, has led to many dysfunctional church families. However, who can blame the church when the primary caregiver, the shepherd, keeps changing every two to five years? In my mind, that is like a family having to deal with a new mother in the home every two to five years. We would all expect the family to be dysfunctional. Mom can make or break a home. Unfortunately for the church, this is also true when it comes to pastors. When pastors come and go "as the Spirit leads," it has a damaging effect on the church.

I have written this book because I desire to see pastors stay longer in their church ministries, because I love the church and strongly believe that this is what will be best for the church. I believe that church members can help in this matter if they understand why pastors leave a church. Since some leave due to the stresses of ministry on the pastor, his wife and family, the church needs to understand how it can care for the caregiver.

I have been a pastor for over twenty-seven years. My first position was as a student while I was in Bible College. This lasted for the duration of my studies, three years. After college, I became a youth pastor for two years. I then served as senior pastor in one charge for seven years and my present charge for over seventeen years. I am the son of a missionary pastor. My father was a pastor on the mission field for seventeen years. I learned many great things about ministry from him.

This book is not a scientific study or an exhaustive evaluation of pastoral ministry, but rather an expression of a pastor's heart as I share what I have observed about pastors and church life. Many of the stories shared in this book are from my personal experience and my observations as a pastor.

Before we get into the book, I need to define what I mean by "primary caregiver". When I describe the pastor as the primary caregiver, I do not mean that the pastor has to hold every person's hand through every situation. For example, the pastor does not have to pray over you as if his prayer holds more power than that of anyone else in the church. If a deacon or someone who is part of the church cares for you, you have been cared for by the church. You do not always require a visit from the pastor. If someone from the church visits you, then the church has visited you.

I am the second youngest of twelve. My mom was a great mother but, at the same time, my older siblings provided much of my care. For instance, I do not remember my mom bathing me, while I do remember my two oldest sisters caring for me in that way. In a healthy church, the family members help each other and receive that help, as from God, through the church. The pastor is not the church and cannot care for everyone, not even in a small church of fifty. I have personally tried and come close to burnout.

Therefore, by primary caregiver, I mean the shepherd who guides by the Word of God and upholds the people of God in prayer. The caregiver seeks to care for the needs of the church by including the family of God in ministering to itself.

I have written this book from a male pastor's perspective as that is the position my church holds to be biblical; nevertheless, I do believe that this book will help church members of all denominations understand the pressures on their pastor no matter what their gender may be.

CONTENTS

- The lifeboat is about to sink
- Discouragements

Chapter 5: **HELPING YOUR PASTOR STAY LONG**

- Pastors need encouragement
- Praying for your pastor and letting him know
- Encouraging your pastor to take time off
- Helping your pastor take care of his health
- Allowing your pastor to develop his skills

Chapter 6: **THE PASTOR'S WIFE NEEDS HER HUSBAND**

- The most important person in your pastor's life is his wife
- The pastor's wife must come before the church
- Happy wife, happy ministry
- The pastor's wife needs her husband

Chapter 7: **THE PASTOR'S WIFE NEEDS GOOD RELATIONSHIPS IN THE BODY**

- The loneliest person in the church
- What does a good relationship look like?
- Why you want her to have at least one good relationship in the church

Chapter 8: **THE PASTOR'S FAMILY MUST COME FIRST**

- The pastor's family must come before the church
- What does it profit a pastor to...lose his kids?

- Help your pastor put his family first

Chapter 9: **THE PASTOR'S KIDS ARE JUST KIDS**

- That is the pastor's kid
- Many parents or children of the church?
- Do not ruin your dad's ministry

Chapter 10: **FREE YOUR PASTOR TO SERVE WITH JOY**

- Three things that will hinder your pastor
- Three things that will help your pastor

Chapter 11: **FOR PASTORS ONLY**

- Study and pray
- Exercise is good for the body and the soul
- Your spouse is priority number one
- Do not lose your kids
- Develop other leaders who can take over
- Be watchful for burnout
- Develop good friends
- Sharpen your skills
- The adult child of a dysfunctional church

Chapter 1

PASTORING IS MORE LIKE BEING A HOMEMAKER THAN A CEO

IF THE PASTOR IS THE CEO

We hear a lot about church growth and I do believe that God desires to see the church grow. However, this emphasis on church growth has led us to expect the senior pastor to be the CEO of the church instead of the shepherd. While this model might be effective for numerical growth, it has a devastating impact on the health of the church over the long haul. Shepherds were never called to be the CEOs of the church.

In this chapter, I will raise the question: What happens to the church if the senior pastor is the CEO and not the primary caregiver or shepherd? I will demonstrate from Scripture why I believe the model of leadership expected of a pastor is more like that of a homemaker than that of a CEO. I will also explore how these two different leadership styles affect a local church over the long haul.

First, if the pastor is the CEO, he is responsible to the shareholders of the company. In the church, the board of elders, deacons and ultimately, the church members, are the shareholders. While this model may sound reasonable to many, it makes the church primarily a business, and we know what shareholders value in a business – the bottom line. In business, every decision is based on measurable success. Measuring success in the church is not a bad thing as long as the Bible, not a business principle, is the standard. If a pastor considers himself the CEO, he will tend to focus on keeping the shareholders happy, which will lead to one of two approaches:

- Maintain the status quo: Do not dare offend the shareholders

- Move forward: Bigger is better at all costs

However, in both cases, the focus is on pleasing man. What if the status quo or moving forward is not what God wants? Conflicting ideologies result: business versus Biblical values. Who will win? Most often business will win because we must, at all costs, keep the shareholders happy.

Another major problem with the pastor as CEO model that always caused me to question its wisdom is the idea that we can move pastors around at will, firing them if they do not perform well after two years, and hiring someone else who will achieve numerically measurable results. This movement is devastating to the health of the church family. Why does a move every two to five years have such a negative impact on the church? CEOs move around all the time; there are slight adjustments in the process, but business goes on. When pastors move around, however, it is as if the life has been ripped out of the church, which for some churches, takes years to recover from. It is worth noting that some churches never do.

A third concern I have with the pastor as CEO model is that it has led pastors to view their calling as a job. They feel justified leaving one church for a bigger church with larger wages, or because they have had enough of Mr. Ornery's shenanigans and Mrs. Complainer's criticism. They can leave a church falling apart behind them because they have moved on to what appears to be more exciting or more fruitful ministry opportunities. They may also feel they deserve better.

Furthermore, Paul has something to say about the CEO model in pastoring:

> For we never came with flattering speech, as
> you know, nor with a pretext for greed – God
> is witness – nor did we seek glory from men,

either from you or from others, even though as apostles of Christ, we might have asserted our authority. But we proved to be gentle among you, as a nursing mother tenderly cares for her own children. Having so fond an affection for you, we were well pleased to impart to you not only the gospel of God but also our own lives, because you had become very dear to us. For you recall brethren, our labor and hardship, how working night and day so as not to be a burden to any of you, we proclaimed to you the gospel of God. You are witnesses, and so is God, how devoutly and uprightly and blamelessly we behaved toward you believers; just as you know how we were exhorting and encouraging and imploring each one of you as a father would his own children, so that you would walk in a manner worthy of the God who calls you into His own kingdom and glory (1 Thessalonians 2:5-12).[1]

I love this passage because it reveals Paul's heart toward pastoring God's people. Paul was a strong leader, a get-the-job-done, no-nonsense kind of person. However, even more notably, this passage emphasizes what Paul did not do. Even though he was entitled to because he was one of the great apostles of Jesus Christ, he did not come as a CEO or the director of a business. He did not come with greed or strive to make a name for himself. He did not come with a polished program that would get results.

In contrast to the CEO mentality, Paul came to them as a nursing mother. I am not sure what picture that gives you, but my wife and I have six children: four biological, and

---

[1] All Scripture quotations are taken from the *New American Standard Bible.*

two through the foster care system. When my wife nursed our four, she did not give them orders nor demand results. She gently and lovingly caressed them as they nursed; this was a time for her to bond with our children as no one else could, not even myself, their father. If she had come in like a CEO, the results would have been far different. The bonding time would have been lost and there would have been tension and stress instead of nurturing and peace.

Furthermore, Paul explains why acting as the CEO does not work in the church. As a CEO, a pastor must stay at arm's length from the subordinates or pastoral staff because he may need to fire them. He would also need to keep himself at arm's length from the shareholders or church board and members so as to not allow emotions to get in the way of good policies – policies that will lead to success.

Paul says "no" to this kind of thinking. Instead, he describes his fond affection for the church. A pastor must become emotionally involved with the people God has called him to serve. Paul further emphasizes this point when he says, "we were well pleased to impart to you not only the gospel of God but also our own lives." A CEO will impart his wisdom, but his personal life is just that – personal. In contrast, it is vital that pastors impart not just the gospel, but also their very own personal lives. Paul explains why: "because you had become very dear to us." One problem I see in the church today is pastors who have little or no heart for God's people. Perhaps at one time they did, but they lost it because of hurt and disappointment. I understand that; I have experienced my fair share of hurt in the ministry as a pastor and have been disappointed after pouring my life into someone only to see him or her walk away. Yet as a pastor, I cannot afford to lose a heart for God's people, no matter what. If a pastor loses a heart for God's people, then he loses his effectiveness in ministry.

Finally, Paul reminds the church of how hard he worked and how much he suffered just to minister to them. A

CEO may work hard, but the motive behind all he does is based on the need to produce results. While Paul was certainly interested in results, he describes the type of results he was striving for in verses 11-12. First, we see the motivation behind all the hard work and suffering Paul experienced was his love for God's people. I believe that the key to a successful ministry is the heart pastors have for the people of God, the Church.

Second, Paul worked to see each believer live in a manner worthy of God. This is a high call to place on a pastor – to measure his success not by the number of professions of faith, the size of the church or the quantity of church programs, but rather by how the people of God entrusted in his care live before God. Are they living better today than they did this time last year? Here again, Paul does not use the CEO mentality of giving orders and setting deadlines or approving agendas and projecting the future direction of the organization. The organization does not concern Paul the most. Paul is instead concerned with the individual, using the illustration of a father to describe the role of a pastor – a family man who has enough time and energy to pour into his children's lives and thereby exhort, encourage, and implore them to live right.

IMAGINE IF MOM ACTED LIKE A CEO

What would your life have been like if your mom acted like a CEO? What if she had treated your family like a business? What if every two to five years you had ended up with a new mom? What effect would that have had on your life?

If Mom acted like a CEO instead of a caregiver, when Johnny came home with an A minus on his report card, how would she respond? As CEO, she would most likely respond with a question that would focus on why he did not get an A plus. After all, she provided him with a tutor and all the resources he needed to get the job done well. If Mom acted

12

like a CEO and Sally came home with second prize in the city championships for figure skating, Mom would question why she paid for all those extra lessons if they did not achieve the desired first place.

I thank the Lord that my mother did not act like a CEO, nor did the mother of my children. Mom is the primary caregiver. When Johnny comes home with an A minus or even a C plus, Mom is there to greet him with a smile and words of encouragement. She would certainly celebrate an A minus. When Sally comes home with a second place ribbon, Mom is there to sing her praises, not put her down.

So how do these examples relate to pastoring? If the pastor acts like the CEO of the church, then he will focus on outward results, often missing the more important growth of God's people. For example, if someone was struggling to run the youth ministry well, the natural tendency would be to pull that person out, instead of coming alongside him and helping him grow. The CEO would consider a thriving youth program more important than helping the struggling youth worker grow in his walk with God as well as in his ministry. Often, the pastor's attitude is, "I have given him all he needs to get the job done well. I bought the best youth program out there and even took time to train him. If he cannot get the job done, then let him move over and have someone else try." Sometimes it is necessary to retire workers from a particular program; however, a willingness to give some tender loving care as a mother, or exhorting and encouraging and imploring as a father will have better results even if it takes longer to get the job done.

If the pastor sees himself as the primary caregiver, he will focus more on the people and God's work in their lives than on outward results. Although someone may be struggling to get the job done, the caregiver will not remove that person, but instead help him improve. Eventually he will get the job done well; the result of this approach is maturity and spiritual growth. With the CEO mentality, this approach does not work: how can the pastor measure this type of growth and how can he report it? After all, he must have something to report to the shareholders or church board and members, especially if his job is on the line every two to five years based on the results.

A home where Mom acts as a CEO, moving on at will to bigger and better situations or where she could be fired if her children do not achieve an A plus or first place, would be disastrous and undesirable. Mom must consider herself the primary caregiver because that will lead to the best results – a healthy home, producing mature grown-ups.

In the same way, a church culture where the pastor acts as a CEO, freely moving on every two to five years to something bigger and better or where he could be fired when church programs do not achieve the results everybody wants, would be disastrous and undesirable. A pastor must see himself as the primary caregiver because that will lead to the best results – a healthy church, producing mature grown-ups in the faith.

THE JOB IS NEVER FINISHED

The homemakers reading this book will relate to these next two sections. For those who are not homemakers, ask the homemaker in your home to explain, as I feel certain she will be able to enlighten you.

Unlike the job of a CEO, a homemaker's job is never finished. The CEO has deadlines he can sign off on once met. Homemakers do not have that luxury. Even when the laundry is done, the kitchen all cleaned up, supper in the oven and everything seems in order, it is amazing how there is always something else that needs Mom's attention. There is always something needing cleaning, straightening out or washing; homemaking is a never-ending job.

Pastoring is similar. As a pastor, for the most part, I do the same jobs repeatedly. I get one sermon prepared and I am on to the next. I meet with someone for counselling and then I am on to the next ministry opportunity. Every week brings much of the same. I am not complaining because I love it. In pastoring, there are weeks when I am overwhelmed and there are weeks when things have settled down.

When a pastor acts as the CEO, he can easily become discouraged because much of what he does is not measurable. How much time should he spend in study, visiting, counselling, and administration? What will produce the best results? How can he measure the results? Most of these questions do not have a definitive answer.

If I were to approach the pastorate from a CEO's perspective and be results driven, then I might spend more time studying than visiting in order to be at the top of my game on Sunday mornings to impress the shareholders and attract new ones. Alternatively, I might spend more time visiting and neglect my preparation time if I see networking as the best way to achieve the desired results.

However, when a pastor sees himself as the primary caregiver, ministry is different. There are times he must drop everything he planned to do and simply meet the needs of someone God places in his path on that given day. The main difference between this approach and the CEO's is the sense of fulfilment and satisfaction. The CEO sees these interruptions as problems, while the pastor sees them as opportunities.

Jesus is a great example of seeing opportunity:

> Now when Jesus heard about John, He withdrew from there in a boat to a secluded place by Himself; and when the people heard of this, they followed Him on foot from the cities. When He went ashore, He saw a large crowd, and felt compassion for them and healed their sick (Matthew 14:13-14).

Jesus was tired and grieving. He was ready for some alone time. He could very well have said, "I need time to myself and I have every right to have this alone time. A close friend and family member just died and I am over-worked." No one would have criticized Him for that. Yet Jesus felt compassion and healed the sick. It is important to note that Jesus did not just heal sick people. He did not just do the job. A CEO may do the job. The issue of feeling compassion moves the work from a job to a ministry of love and care.

Therefore, like Jesus, a pastor may be tired and have different plans for the day or evening when a real need arises. The pastor will put aside the plans for the day to care for the flock. He does this because he feels compassion for the people of God, not because it is his job.

There does need to be a balance here though, for sometimes pastors do struggle with being workaholics for Jesus. I heard Dr. Joseph Stowell address this issue at a conference a number of years ago. He talked about how he would often run out on family events like birthdays and special dinners. He did this because someone from his flock, for whom he had great compassion, called for help. In time, however, he needed to deal with this constant demand on his time. He learned to balance his time by asking some basic questions to determine if it was a real "I need to leave right now and tend to the flock" situation or more of a "here are some Scriptures, let's pray and then call me at the office tomorrow" situation. I will expand on this topic when I discuss the pastor's family in Chapters 6 and 8.

THERE IS LITTLE TO NO THANKS

Pastors do not have a time clock. They are on call 24/7. Every week there are things that need to be finished. Many of the things pastors do go unnoticed simply because they are completed.

It is like having Mom around. When was the last time you noticed and said "thank you" to your mom for washing the socks, vacuuming the floors, dusting the bookshelves, or chopping the carrots? We do not even notice these things.

However, if she did not do these things, you would ask her about the socks, wonder why your allergies are bothering you so much and complain that the carrots are too long to fit in your mouth!

When it comes to pastoring, many unseen jobs are only noticed when they are not done, such as visiting. In smaller churches, the pastor is often left doing many unseen jobs like the bulletin, announcements or even general maintenance of the facilities. No one really thinks about who completes these tasks, as long as they are done.

There are many things that a pastor never receives a thankful mention for, although many times he is criticized for things he missed. Often, a pastor hears a "thank you" as he stands at the door after church on Sunday mornings. People thank him for his morning message, but sometimes people use that time to set their pastor straight on something he said in the sermon. Why not arrange an appointment if it really needs to be addressed?

Just as Mom is not thanked for the everyday things that she does, things that we have come to expect, it is always nice to take the time to say "thank you Mom." While it is great to do something for Mom on Mother's Day, it is even more special when it is done unexpectedly.

Similarly, October is observed as Pastor Appreciation Month. It is a great idea, but care must be taken to not wait until October to appreciate your pastor. Maybe he needs to know you appreciate him today. If your pastor has done something that you really appreciate, why not let him know? Write a card, send an email or take him out for coffee. Go ahead and use your imagination.

Finally, if you are a pastor, it is important to remember that God is our rewarder and all we do, we do for Him. Also, for how we serve in secret, God will reward us some day in public.

Chapter 2

PASTORS DO NOT WORK FOR A LIVING

A ONE-DAY JOB

Some pastors may not like the title of this chapter, but be patient and remember that I am a pastor as well. I have a plaque in my office that says, "I am not paid to preach. I am given an allowance so that I am free to preach." The church I am currently serving gives me an allowance on the first day of each month. When I arrived here on the first day, before I did anything, they gave me what I would need to take care of my family. Some will ask, "What is the difference and does it really matter?" I have chosen to make it matter because it subtly communicates the truth that I am not paid for what I have done but set free to do ministry as God leads.

I have heard all the jokes about how nice it must be to work only on Sundays. People often have little understanding of what a pastor does. I have found that there are two groups within the church. There are those who underestimate what a pastor does and there are those who embellish what a pastor's life is like.

My mother in-law told some of my wife's siblings that my wife wrote my sermons and all I did was preach them on Sundays. My wife and I have often laughed about that idea because, in many ways, that would be more challenging than if I just wrote them myself.

GETTING READY FOR THAT ONE-DAY JOB

Most pastors spend a fair amount of time in sermon preparation. At the start, he must determine what topic he will be preaching. For some pastors, that is a week-by-week task. If they are preaching through a book of the Bible, verse by verse, then the topic is naturally the next passage, but they still need to break the verses down into bite-sized pieces. If they take the more topical approach then they face the challenge of finding a new topic each week. Some pastors plan their topics a month or even six months ahead. Personally, I sit down with my elders to plan sermon topics and series for the whole year. Some may wonder about the leading of the Holy Spirit in this approach. I have to affirm that there have been many times when people have expressed how they needed that word right then. It has also meant that I could say on occasion that I did not pick a particular message in response to what had been going on in the past week but that the elders actually chose it nine months ago. This helps people to feel secure in trusting that God was speaking to them rather than me using the pulpit as an opportunity to preach at them.

Once your pastor knows what topic to preach on, he then must research the topic, reading and studying the text, the background of the text, word studies, and what other people think about the text. This is like the preparation work in the kitchen: cutting up all the vegetables, peeling the potatoes, tenderizing the meat or skinning and deboning the chicken.

Following the bulk of the studying, the pastor must let the information simmer. When is the last time you had homemade soup? I do not mean soup out of a can, because almost anyone can open a can and heat it up, but homemade soup – that is the good stuff. What makes homemade soup so good is the simmering. All the flavours mix and mingle, which is what sets homemade apart from all the rest. That is true of a good sermon as well. It needs to simmer on the back burner for a day or two. When your pastor has had the time to study and then think the information over and let it all come together, it is amazing what he will get.

Because a pastor's life can be so busy, sometimes all the congregation receives is canned goods from Sermons-R-Us. While there are times for canned, you do not want a steady diet of that. It will give you spiritual heartburn. That is why it is important you give your pastors the time to let their sermons simmer, time to meditate on the sermon.

After it simmers, he must flesh it all out on paper or the computer screen. This is when your pastor, under the direction of the Holy Spirit, puts down all the things that his studying has lead him to believe about the text or topic. He may write out his sermon word for word or put it in point form. Some have copious notes while others have very few. This sets the stage for the presentation on Sunday morning, similar to putting the food in the serving dishes before you bring it to the table. Do you just use the pots and pans, or place it in a dish with garnish to dress it up? How should he present it?

Throughout this preparation, an important ingredient is prayer. If your pastor is conscientious about preaching and teaching God's word, it only makes sense that he consult the author of the Word during the whole process of studying, simmering, and presenting.

MINISTERING IS NOT WORKING

What does your pastor do for a living? Does he work or minister? People are often confused by this question. Sometimes people will look at their pastor and wonder what he is doing on the golf course on Wednesday morning or why he is at the local coffee shop again. Does he not have any work to do? Should he not be in the office in case they need to call for counselling? How can their pastor come to their house in the middle of the day, and sit and have a coffee with them? I have had people from the church ask me when I normally take my day off so we can go golfing or so they can have my family over for dinner.

What is work? According to the Encarta Dictionary, work is defined as "time spent at place of employment or the time that somebody spends carrying out his or her job."[2] The pastor's workplace is not solely the office. Yes, pastors need to spend time there in sermon preparation and administrative

---

[2] "work," The Encarta ® World English Dictionary © & (P), 1998-2005.

duties, but a pastor also needs to build into peoples' lives. It is another facet of ministry, the aspect of his "job" people often struggle with because he seems to be having too much fun.

Is the homemaker shirking her duties if she goes to the park with her children instead of washing the floor or folding the laundry? Granted, if she does not complete her housework on a regular basis there may be a problem, but in the end, what is the more important matter: folding the laundry or building a relationship with her children? The same is true of the pastorate. Certainly, there are day-to-day tasks to be completed, but building relationships is more important than any other issue. Think of a youth pastor for a moment. He may have the best program possible but no relationship with the youth. Will he be effective in changing the lives of the youth just because he has a great program? No. The same is true for the senior pastor who may be very well prepared for the Sunday morning sermon, but if he does not know the people, how effective will he be at truly caring for them?

Ministry happens everywhere and in every setting. As a pastor, when I visit, go for a coffee, or go golfing, I am always in the process of building into peoples' lives. Sometimes I achieve this goal formally and sometimes informally, but either way, the time I spend with God's people is never wasted. Remember, ministry is not work; it is building into people's lives. Once I had someone ask me when I was visiting with him if I was working. What he meant was whether I considered spending time with him as work? My answer was both yes and no. I was doing my job, ministering to the flock, but at the same time, I was enjoying myself. In other words, it was not a chore. So when you see your pastor at the coffee shop with someone from the church or community or maybe even reading a book, do not assume he is neglecting his duties. He may be very much involved in ministry.

AN ACCURATE JOB DESCRIPTION

If you were to survey any local church with the simple question, "What should your pastor be doing," the list of responses would be diverse. Some would say the pastor should follow the example of the apostles as described in Acts 6:4, which states, "we will devote ourselves to prayer and to the ministry of the word." However, this response raises the question, are pastors really apostles? While we could probably say that Peter was both a pastor and an apostle, this is not necessarily true of the pastor today. I believe this example could be too narrow as some pastors could use this example as an excuse to avoid spending time in ministry beyond the pulpit.

Some pastors do need more preparation time than others do. However, there is more to pastoring than just preaching exceptionally well. Pastors need to connect with their people for times of fellowship and be available during times of need. If all Mom did was make food and clean the house, the family would wither up and die. In fact, you do not need a mom for that – all you need is a maid. If all the pastor does is preach well, the church will not survive. You do not need a pastor for that, just a satellite uplink, or a hired gun – someone with a few silver bullet sermons. The pastor's job description is more than just preaching. The pastor is called to care for the flock, and in every church setting, that care will look different.

Be careful not to overburden your pastor. Recognize what the body can do for itself and do not expect your pastor to do what the body can do. My current congregation has many strengths. It does well when it comes to welcoming newcomers and visiting amongst themselves so I can focus on other things that will help care for the church family. It is kind of like the children knowing how to do their own laundry. Why would they expect Mom to do laundry for them? She can focus on something else that will better help the family. There may be times when she will still do the children's laundry, but not as a rule. Good mothers do not want their children to lose sight of what they can do for themselves.

To determine its pastor's job description, each church needs to look at its own strengths. Based on those strengths, determine together with your pastor how he can best minister in your local setting. At times, he may very well do some of the things like visiting, but if visiting is your congregation's strength, it would be foolish to expect that to be your pastor's primary role. If your church is strong on evangelism, then maybe his primary role should be discipleship or visitation. Do not be afraid to break the mould; dare to try something new and different.

IF PASTORS WORKED FOR A LIVING

I remember my dad telling me a story about a pastor who did not attend a funeral for one of the church members because it was on his day off. This probably says it all – if your pastor views ministry as a job, you have a problem.

Ministry is a calling. There are no time limits or restrictions on ministry. A job is very different. It is nine to five, five days a week. This schedule works in business but not in a church family because people do not wait until 9am to get hurt or for a crisis to happen in their lives. I mentioned previously that my wife and I have six children. As they were growing up, inevitably, one of our children would get sick, usually late at night. Imagine what our home would be like if my wife and I told our child it was after hours and to go back to bed and call us in the morning.

If a pastor views his ministry as a job, he will inevitably put himself first instead of his flock. In the example I gave in Chapter 1, Jesus demonstrated His attitude toward ministry. Yes, He was tired and needed rest, but He felt compassion and ministered to the people. He did not just do the job. He felt genuine compassion for the people, as reflected in how he ministered. If your pastor gets to the place where he is just doing a job, do not fire him or run him out of town, instead pray for him and encourage him to take some time away to get refreshed and spiritually renewed.

If you are a pastor and your ministry has become just a job to you, do not leave the church. I know at times loving God's people is hard, but you cannot afford not to love them. Going to another church will not solve the problem. Every church I have been in has the same challenging personalities in them somewhere, and they will eventually come to the surface in the new church. Seek to be renewed in your spirit, and do all you can to have God rekindle the fire of His love in you for God's people where you are.

Chapter 3

NOT EVERY PASTOR IS A CHEF IN THE PULPIT

SUBSTANCE OR FLAIR?

There was a time when many people considered eating out a treat. Often people only ate out once or twice a year, perhaps for a special occasion or while on vacation. However, today eating out is almost a norm. We frequent fancier, more expensive restaurants more often today than our parents or grandparents would have and we tend to grab bites to eat at the food court while we are out shopping more often than they did. This has also become a reality spiritually. We can eat out every day at the food court of the spiritual mall of Christian programming from our satellite dishes, internet connections, satellite radios, and iPhones.

I like Christian programming; it does a lot of good. However, we face some issues today because of Christian programming and the internet that my father, as a pastor, and the people of his congregation, did not face. Since we can listen to great preaching at any time of the day, anywhere we like, even on our iPhones, it is easy for the congregation to compare their pastor to all kinds of fantastic preachers. This has led to greater pressure on the local pastors to perform better and has caused many parishioners to become dissatisfied with their local pastor's preaching abilities.

My mom was a good cook in her own right. She made the best meatballs and stewing beef mixture. It was great! She made soup twice a day because my dad had to have soup for lunch and supper, before the main dish. Her cooking was not fancy. It was meat, potatoes, vegetables, and dessert. She had eleven children to feed every day and often there would be a guest as well, so she was more concerned with substance than she was with presentation.

When it comes to preaching, some pastors are more of your meat and potatoes kind of preachers. There is a lot to chew on but it is not very fancy. They do not use humour or interesting stories. They just get right to the Word and put it all out there on the table for you to get your fill. Some pastors will give you lots of flair, but there is not much to it. I compare it to a meal I had at a fancy restaurant once: a huge plate with all kinds of frills, four beans, two small round potatoes and a small piece of meat. It looked great, tasted fantastic, but left me completely dissatisfied and wanting more.

What do you do if you have a pastor whose preaching does not meet your needs? Many people move on to the next church and hope for the best. However, there is another answer, maybe even more than one answer. Why not examine your own heart? Is the problem with your pastor or with you? Profound preaching to one person is often only basic to another, so it could just be a matter of taste. It could also be an issue of arrogance in your heart or an unteachable attitude.

What if the problem does in fact lie with the pastor? Maybe his meat and potatoes lack the gravy and flavour to keep you interested. Perhaps his presentation is great, but it does not fill you and you are always left feeling there was nothing of substance. Then what? You can always supplement your meals; there are places to find both substance as well as flair. Read good books or go online and listen to a good sermon by someone with more flair or with the substance you want and need. However, be careful in the process that you do not develop a critical spirit and be even more careful that you do not spread a critical spirit throughout the church family.

EVERYONE ENJOYS A HOME-COOKED MEAL

Home-cooked meals are always the best, even if they lack flair, because of what they accomplish for the family. They bring us together. When I was growing up, the supper meal was the time when all thirteen of us gathered around the table. I do not remember every meal my mom made, but I do remember being together, even from a very young age. I fondly remember the good times we had at the supper table.

If your pastor is not a chef with flair, look at the substance, and choose to chew on the meat of the Word presented. This may mean that you will need to do some of your own work. Take what he provides and dig deeper yourself. More importantly look around and see how the meal is affecting others in the family. Choose to see how God is using the meat and potato message to cause others in the family to grow and thank Him.

There may be an opportunity to give your pastor a good book or a CD on developing his skills as a preacher. You must be extremely careful with how and when you give the gift. I had someone once give me a great book, but because of whom he was and the timing of the gift, I never read it. I felt that the book was meant as an attack. It was not until years later that a friend told me about this great book. Then I read it and found it to be helpful.

A final word to pastors: we need to be real and accept that just like a professional baseball player who has played all his life needs to better his skills, we also need to better our skills, even if we have been preaching for years. Just as the baseball player should not be offended if someone comes to him with a suggestion on how to improve his game, we should not get defensive, even if the person has never preached a sermon in his or her life. I have been preaching for many years and recently my wife suggested a CD series by Timothy Keller on preaching. My staff and I listened to the series and began applying some of his principles. Just halfway through the CDs, two people commented that they had noticed the preaching had changed. Oddly enough, they were compliments. It is so important to continue to grow as a pastor.

GO OUT FOR DINNER OCCASIONALLY

There are times that going out for dinner is nice and may be even necessary. My family loves to tell the story of how I once ruined supper. In fact, at times, they make it sound like all my cooking is bad. One time I made homemade soup, and as usual, I took whatever leftovers were in the refrigerator and added those things into the soup. Usually it tastes very good, but this particular time I decided to be creative and put some oatmeal in the soup to make it creamy and more filling. It was so bad that even our dog would not eat it, so we ordered pizza.

There have been times as a pastor, that I knew that my sermon was a "let's eat out" kind of meal. I blew it because I did not put in enough time and energy or I did not let it simmer in my heart and mind long enough. Whatever the reason, in the end, people were left wanting. At times like that it may be good and even necessary for the parishioner to eat out by listening to a sermon online or on a DVD.

Sometimes it is just nice to go out for dinner. This is true spiritually as well. Go to a good conference or order a good set of DVDs covering a topic of interest. Downloading something onto you iPhone or MP3 player can be very enjoyable and helpful as well.

EATING OUT CAN CAUSE DISSATISFACTION

However, one of the problems with constantly eating out is what it can do to our taste buds. On an episode of *Corner Gas*, a sitcom based in rural Saskatchewan, the main character, Brent Butt was introduced to the finer cuisine of The Ruby. Since becoming acquainted with this new flavour, he was unable to enjoy his usual favorites chili dogs. His taste buds had changed to the point that even one of his favorite dishes that his mother made left him wanting something better.

Spiritually, when we go out to dine, we can become

so dissatisfied with the home-cooked meal that we once so much enjoyed, that we become critical. The very thing that at one time was a blessing, is now a curse. So yes, go out to eat, and thank God for great men and women who can capably communicate God's word. However, do not compare your pastor to these people. Your pastor has skills that God has blessed him with to serve in your particular church ministry, so thank God for your pastor and the gifts God has given him.

Chapter 4

HOW TO RUN YOUR PASTOR OUT OF TOWN

WHAT REALLY HURTS YOUR PASTOR

There are certain things that hurt moms deeply, so it would be good for the whole family, as well as for Mom, to avoid those things. This is true of any caregiver because they become emotionally connected to those they care for regularly. When those very people hurt them, the hurt is often more intense and more damaging than if it came from a mere acquaintance.

For example, you should avoid criticizing Mom's ability to cook or to keep a clean house to avoid undermining her confidence and damaging your relationship. You should also avoid criticizing her person, the way she dresses, or how she carries herself. Personal attacks are probably the most devastating issues of all. Your pastor, in many ways, faces the same hurts when you lash out at him. Because he has compassion for you, he has become emotionally connected to you; you are more than a mere acquaintance.

Some may wonder why I would mention this topic. Could this not give people ammunition to hurt their pastor? Yes, I suppose it could. At the same time, I feel this issue should be addressed for two reasons: first, to help people avoid unintentionally hurting their pastor and second, to help pastors protect themselves from unnecessary pain. As a pastor, I have taught many marriage courses. Some people use the very things intended to help their marriage to hurt their spouse and harm their marriage. So examining what hurts your pastor could be risky, but the intent is that you use this information for good.

A number of things can really hurt your pastor. Personal attacks are never good for your pastor, especially when they are about issues that he can do little or nothing about. Those kinds of attacks go right to the heart. Even worse than personal attacks are attacks on the pastor's family, their spouse, or children.

What do these attacks look like? They are unfair criticisms and negative comments meant to bring the pastor's credibility into question such as personal criticism about the pastor's weight, clothes, or certain aspects of his personality. I recall one instance when someone came to my office and told me I was too strong of a leader, too opinionated, too dogmatic, and that I was going to destroy the church. That very same week, someone else came to my office and told me that I was too soft of a leader, and too wishy-washy, and that I was going to destroy the church. I learned then that I needed to be the person God made me to be; I had to serve to the best of my ability, and let God take care of the rest.

In addition, often the pastor's children's behaviour is used against him. The criticism is that if the pastor cannot manage his children, then he should not be a pastor. People will even quote Scripture to prove their point. However, they forget two things: first, when a child misbehaved in Biblical times, the father could do with his child as he wished; there was no excuse for disrespectful children, where as today one has to be very careful when it comes to discipline. Second, in Biblical times there were no teenagers. You were either a child under your parents' control or an adult. For instance, boys were able to get married at the age of fourteen and girls at the age of twelve. Therefore, what should a pastor do in today's society when he has a child living at home into their mid to late twenties? At what point is the child to be held responsible for his or her own actions?

To make a primary argument against a pastor's qualifications based on his children as young adults is suspect. In addition, what is the definition of a well-managed household? Every family has an aspect of dysfunction in it. Is your own family the measuring stick for your pastor and his family? In Chapter 9, I will focus on the effects of this type of criticism on the pastor's children. Therefore, may I encourage you, rather than criticize your pastor's family, pray for them and do all you can to encourage them.

Another way to drive your pastor away is to question his ability to interpret Scripture. This can undermine the pastor's confidence and even cause him to leave the ministry altogether. This would be like saying to your mom that you are a lousy cook just because she burnt the potatoes once or twice. I am not talking about a good discussion and a healthy disagreement; most pastors would love to have a healthy argument on Scriptures that are open for debate. I am talking about challenging his overall ability.

I remember one case where I was so rattled, I had to go to several pastors and ask them if I was completely out to lunch on my interpretation of Scripture regarding a particular subject. It took me two weeks before I regained my confidence, and I do not have an inferiority complex, I am normally a very confident person. I have often thought about pastors I know who already lack confidence and how much more devastating this would have been for them. There is a better way. Be polite, agree to disagree, recognize that you and your pastor obviously may have strong views. The fact that you cannot agree does not mean that your pastor is unable to interpret the Scriptures. In reality, your pastor may feel that you are the one who lacks the interpretive skills, and considering that, in most cases your pastor has had years of training along with practice which you may not have had, he may be right!

Finally, Proverbs 10:1 says, "a foolish son is a grief to his mother." As a mother is grieved by a foolish son, so is a pastor grieved by a foolish parishioner. After he has poured his heart and soul into someone, only to have that person walk away from the faith or turn on him and condemn his ministry is heartbreaking. Sometimes it is not even that the person walks away from the faith or turns on the pastor, but simply walks away from the pastor after he has poured so much time and energy into that life. Hebrews 13:17 states, "Obey your leaders and submit to them, for they keep watch over your souls as those who will give an account. Let them do this with joy and not with grief, for this would be unprofitable for you." When pastors serve with grief, they will not last.

WHY PASTORS LEAVE A CHURCH

Why do moms leave the home? Often it is because of a lack of communication, some form of abuse, or that they just cannot handle the situation any more. Some pastors may not like what I am about to say, yet it needs to be said. Most pastors do not leave their church because of the Lord. Do not get me wrong, there are times that God moves a pastor from one ministry to another, but more often than not, pastors move and use God as a scapegoat.

If God is moving pastors as often as we claim, then why does it have such a negative effect on the church? This logic would suggest that maybe God does not know what He is doing. Also, why does it often seem that He moves pastors up into larger, more prestigious ministries, and not down into more needy ministries? Finally, why does His moving a pastor so often appear to coincide with problems in the church? As pastors, we must be open and honest with ourselves as well as the church. While this can be risky, and at times hard, it must be done. If problems or problem people in the church are the cause for our leaving, we must be honest about that.

THE TOONIE EFFECT

So why do pastors leave? Often it has to do with one or two people. When pastors get so focused on the problem people, we miss the blessings that God is providing in the ministry. You have Mr. Ornery and Mrs. Complainer. The pastor ends up spending so much time and energy trying to be careful not to set them off that the focus shifts from God and what He is doing, to a point where the pastor cannot see anything but difficulties. I have experienced what it is like to preach with the knowledge that while preaching, I should be careful where I looked when I said certain things. I knew that if I looked in the wrong direction, Mrs. Complainer would think that I was directing my comments straight at her. At the same time, Mr. Ornery would be convinced that my point was about him, even though I was preaching verse by verse through the text. That can be very tiresome and at times very challenging, especially in a smaller congregation where there is more than one or two of these types of people.

If you are Canadian, you could call it the "toonie effect." A toonie is the Canadian two dollar coin, a little larger than a quarter. The toonie effect occurs when someone goes on an excursion to see the Rocky Mountains, brings a toonie with him and holds it at arm's length in front of his face. While everyone around him is amazed by the grandeur and the splendor of God's marvelous work of creation, all he can focus on is the toonie. In church ministry, this happens when the pastor only focuses on the problem people while everyone around him sees all that God is doing. When the pastor resigns, people are shocked by the pastor's decision. They do not see the problems; they see how God is using the pastor and cannot understand why God would move the pastor at this time.

THE LIFEBOAT IS ABOUT TO SINK

When the Titanic went down in 1912, one of the problems the crew faced was that they did not have enough lifeboats to manage all the passengers on board that great unsinkable ship. Pastors often leave a church because of burnout. In the local church, workers are like lifeboats. When there are not enough, the few that are present become overloaded and end up burning out. They have given so much of themselves that they face compassion fatigue, so they leave what feels like a sinking ship.

In my experience as a pastor in a small community, the church I was serving in had grown under my ministry from fifty to about ninety. Then the recession hit and the church declined to about thirty-five because people moved away looking for work. We had a budget of $120 000 which dropped to about $40 000. As people left, ministries lost their workers. I had been raised by a pastor who taught me to never let something fail, but to pick up the slack whenever necessary. As the ministry team diminished, it meant that more and more of the ministry fell on my shoulders. At one point I said to my wife, "I feel like a lifeboat that's going down." When the Titanic sank, the leaders in the lifeboats had to recognize what they could and could not handle. Even though it was hard, they had to get away from the sinking ship and keep their distance despite the fact that people were crying for help.

Pastors, myself included, sometimes can feel that way. After a short time, they are overworked because they do not set appropriate boundaries for themselves. They see leaving and going to a new ministry as a fresh start and often the only answer. This temporarily works, but it does not work well. Just as when people move from marriage to marriage only to run into the same problems time and time again, pastors do the same in their ministry life, moving from church to church only to run into the same problem people, Mr. Ornery and Mrs. Complainer, and bring their own bad habits along with them as well.

DISCURAGEMENTS

While the following issues may seem insignificant, they often contribute to a pastor's discouragement. These are just a few that have certainly discouraged me from time to time. One of those apparently insignificant issues is church attendance. For a pastor who works hard to prepare a message and gets up in the pulpit only to find that many of the church members are not there, can be compared to when Mom works all day to prepare a nice meal for the family only to find that the family has decided to go out for pizza and not told her. We live in a society where poor church attendance is becoming more and more of an issue – people will just not show up. I recognize that people miss because of work, and I understand that the long weekend is a time to get away. However, it becomes discouraging for your pastor when you simply choose to stay home; you are communicating the message to your pastor that the thought, time and energy he put into the message is not important to you. If Mom worked hard to have supper ready and the family did not show up, she would wonder why she even bothered. Most pastors I know are happy to preach to whoever shows up, but that does not mean that people missing the main meal of the week does not hurt their Pastor because it does.

Another of these apparently insignificant issues is voting with your pocket book. If a problem needs to be addressed, please go through the right channels and deal with the issue – do not stop giving. If you stop giving, ask yourself, whom am I giving to? Am I giving to the pastor? Am I giving to a particular church program? Or am I giving to the Lord? If you are giving to the pastor, or to a specific program, then withholding your financial support would make sense if it is not meeting your need. However, please understand that in this approach to giving we run the danger of manipulation, control and making it all about us. We are to be giving to the Lord. We do need to be good stewards of our resources; therefore, if we do not support the pastor or the direction of the church, we have two options: ideally, deal with the issue through the proper channels, or, if all else fails, find a new church family that you can whole-heartedly support. Withholding your finances because you are not happy with your pastor or the direction of the church is not a constructive solution and will contribute to driving your pastor away in an unhealthy way for both the pastor and the church.

The final apparently insignificant issue involves commitment. If you say you are going to do something please do it; as Jesus commands us in Matthew 5:37 to, let your "yes" be yes and your "no" be no. One of the things that I really appreciate about my current ministry is that, for the most part, people are good at this. This is so important because it can really hinder the ministry of the church when people say that they will do something and then just do not show up. Going back to the family illustration, when Mom comes home with the groceries to a counter full of dirty dishes when Johnny said that he would clean them up, how will Mom feel? Just as that would be frustrating for Mom, it is frustrating and discouraging for your pastor when you say yes, but mean no.

Chapter 5

HELPING YOUR PASTOR STAY LONG

PASTORS NEED ENCOURAGEMENT

Some might question why pastors need encouragement. If they were ministering for God, would not that be enough? It is true that we are all to derive our ultimate significance from Christ – pastors and church members as well – so why do pastors need encouragement? The simple answer is that pastors are human, and as humans we all like it when someone says, "You are doing a good job."

There are many reasons why it is important for you to encourage your pastor. One reason is that he often faces unfair criticism. It has been said that most of us need ten "at-a-boys" for every one "you-jerk." When you see your pastor next, chances are he just needs you to say something encouraging because someone has already taken care of the negative. He also needs encouragement because much of a pastor's ministry is behind the scenes. There are matters that nobody knows about, and it is easy for him to get discouraged looking after those daily events. Using the illustration of the homemaker, if no one notices the things that the homemaker has done all day, after a while it gets harder and harder to do the extra things because no one notices anyhow. Eventually someone does notice, but it is in the form of a complaint, which only further discourages the homemaker. As some of the homemaker's significance and value is tied to the home, when the home is not appreciated or is criticized, the homemaker sees this as a comment on her value as a person. In comparison, some of a pastor's value and significance is linked to his ability to pastor well, and when you encourage him, he will do much better. So take time to notice when he has obviously spent lots of time preparing a sermon, helping someone in need or in fellowship with someone.

Encouraging your pastor will help him stay for a long time. If you simply show that you are enjoying a sermon, or agree with what your pastor is teaching, it is amazing what God will do. As a pastor, I have been blessed with a few people like that in each church that I have served. These people loved me and showed me by smiling or nodding their heads in agreement during my sermons. They also thanked me for my message. It was not just the, "Good message, Pastor" on the way out of the service, but a sincere "I really appreciate what you said when you said..." They listened and were responsive.

Some simple ways to encourage your pastor that, while they may seem small, are very significant include attending church every Sunday, supporting the work of the church to the best of your ability, and seeing your church commitments through to the end.

PRAYING FOR YOUR PASTOR AND LETTING HIM KNOW

Paul asked for prayer quite frequently, and he let people know when he had been praying for them. Paul, one of the great apostles, needed people to pray for him, and he openly asked for prayer, meaning he was willing to admit his need of the flock to minister to him as he cared for them. For example, Paul asks the Thessalonians to pray for him on numerous occasions:

"Brethren, pray for us" (1 Thessalonians 5:25).

"Finally brethren, pray for us that the word of the Lord will spread rapidly and be glorified, just as it did also with you" (2 Thessalonians 3:1).

Your pastor needs your care; he needs you to pray for him, not just during difficult days, but every day because Satan seems to attack pastors and their families quite often. Here are some things you can pray in general for your pastor:

- That God will protect your pastor from temptation
- That your pastor will have a good relationship with his wife and children
- That your pastor will have the strength and willpower to live a balanced life
- That your pastor's walk with God will grow deeper and more meaningful

The author of Hebrews also calls us to pray for spiritual leaders:

> Obey your leaders and submit to them, for they keep watch over your souls as those who will give an account. Let them do this with joy and not with grief for this would be unprofitable for you. Pray for us, for we are sure that we have a good conscience, desiring to conduct ourselves honourably in all things (Hebrews 13:17-18).

The point is clear: as your leader, your pastor is doing all he can to be honest and faithful to the call of God in caring for the flock. He may be tempted or weak so he needs prayer, especially in those situations where Mr. Ornery and Mrs. Complainer are concerned. So if you know that there are some people who are extra challenging for your pastor, do double time in lifting him up.

Just a word to the pastors reading this: how can your people pray if they do not know what to pray for? May we as pastors learn from Paul to be vulnerable and let our people know that we need their care. I know that for some this is a very scary thought because someone may use that request for help against you. I have had that happen, but what is the alternative to being open and vulnerable? We may occasionally turn to others outside the church family, but at the same time, Paul saw the ministry as a give and take situation where the body takes care of itself, including the pastor.

In addition, several times in Scripture, Paul demonstrates the principle of telling others that you are praying for them:

> "To this end also we pray for you always, that our God will count you worthy of your calling, and fulfill every desire for goodness and the work of faith with power" (2 Thessalonians 1:11).

> "For this reason also, since the day we heard of it, we have not ceased to pray for you and to ask that you may be filled with the knowledge of His will in all spiritual wisdom and understanding" (Colossians 1:9).

> "...I pray that the fellowship of your faith may become effective through the knowledge of every good thing which is in you for Christ's sake" (Philemon 1:6).

Why would Paul emphasize that he was praying for others? Paul was not trying to attract attention to himself. Paul knew that God would answer his prayer in His own time and as He saw fit; Paul also knew the concept of praying in the privacy of his closet. Paul was not saying this to make himself look good. This was not about Paul. I believe Paul told them that he was praying for them so they would be encouraged. This is a great way to encourage your pastor. Pray for him, and do so in private, and do so knowing that God is God in this situation. Then tell your pastor that you have been praying for him – if you truly have been.

ENCOURAGING YOUR PASTOR TO TAKE TIME OFF

This may seem a little odd to you, especially if you have the feeling that pastors only work one day a week. As I have tried to express in Chapter 2, pastoring is a never-ending "job" because it is not a nine-to-five profession. The word job does not properly describe pastoring. It is ministry, and it is ongoing like the work of a homemaker or caregiver. Many pastors are actively involved in ministry nearly seventy hours per week.

Pastors often struggle with being workaholics because there is no defined workweek. They just keep working away because, after all, it is all for the kingdom of God. Yet some great pastors have paid the horrible price of forsaking their children and spouses because somehow they bought into the idea that "if I take care of God's business, He will take care of mine" even though God has not made this promise.

To help your pastor stay longer, your church should require your pastor to take at least one day off per week and at least two weeks of non-ministry related vacation. This does not include conferences or ministry vacations like going to a camp to serve or speak. Nor should it be a mission's trip. These are not restful for your pastor. I am suggesting true rest and relaxation, get-away-from-it-all type of time off. I would recommend that if you are a board member, you ask your pastor about his time off and encourage him to take it.

I know some pastors that would say this recommendation is nonsense and that they can minister nonstop. Maybe they feel they can, but can their wife and children? Is it good for the family, for their spouse and children, to vacation without them? Pastor, let your flock release you to relax. Remember, Jesus is our great example and He took time to rest and God commands us to rest as He rested.

HELPING YOUR PASTOR TAKE CARE OF HIS HEALTH

Your pastor's health can be a challenging topic as well, because so often we think that health is a personal issue. However, if your pastor's ministry could be limited because he has not taken proper care of himself, that affects everyone in the church family.

To be honest, I have a weight problem and I do work at it, but I could do better. I have had people criticize me for this, which did not help. Weight and health issues in general can be touchy topics at best; therefore, addressing them with your pastor requires a strong friendship in which honesty and accountability have already been established. Dare to build a relationship with your pastor, one in which the two of you can challenge each other. Be careful to make sure you create a friendly and encouraging environment that will foster and promote healthy living. Come alongside your pastor and help him develop healthy habits.

Often because of an over commitment to ministry, a pastor may neglect to go to the gym or feel that it is a waste of time. He may even quote Paul: "...for bodily discipline is only of little profit, but godliness is profitable for all things, since it holds promise for the present life and also for the life to come" (1 Timothy 4:8). While this is true when dealing with eternal things, there are two points to note. First, Paul does not say "of no use" but "of little profit" implying that there is some profit in taking care of one's health. Second, Paul was not addressing the issue of longevity in ministry, but he was dealing with the life hereafter.

Pastors, some of us need to admit that although we may be doing a great job when it comes to what we call spiritual disciplines, we neglect to see that taking care of our health is in some sense a spiritual discipline as well. It could be one that can lengthen our years of usefulness in active church ministry.

ALLOWING YOUR PASTOR TO DEVELOP HIS SKILLS

Finally, a pastor may leave a church if he feels he has brought the church as far as he can. He may feel that he has nothing more to give, so he may look for a new opportunity where he can be used by God to bring a new church family along.

In the homemaker or caregiver illustration, this would be like Mom feeling that she has raised the children well, but now that they are about to become teenagers, it is time for her to move on to a new family with little ones. She plans to raise these new children up to and including grade eight, and then repeat the cycle with yet another family. We would all say this is madness and advise her to find some good books on teenagers or talk to someone who has raised teenagers and develop the skills to deal with teenagers.

Sometimes a pastor can feel that he has exhausted all of his resources, and that he needs to have someone pour into his life. If you want your pastor to stay for a long time, it is important that as a church you give your pastor time to hone his skills. Give him some time off that is not vacation time, but retooling time. This can be accomplished either through conferences, allowing him to take a course through a school of his choice, or supplying him with a book allowance.

For the pastors reading this, we need to recognize that we need further education, even if we are not striving for a doctorate. I think that if we ever feel a need to move on because we do not have the skills that the church we are serving requires, rather than move on, we should consider retooling.

Chapter 6

THE PASTOR'S WIFE NEEDS HER HUSBAND

THE MOST IMPORTANT PERSON IN A PASTOR'S LIFE IS HIS WIFE

When a woman marries a pastor, she holds a unique position. Three things occur once she is married to a pastor:

- She is married to someone she has to share, not just with extended family like most people, but with an enlarged extended family called the church family.
- Her identity could be wrapped up in her position as the wife of the pastor and not in who she is as a person.
- Her voice could be silenced because as she needs to guard what she says to avoid damaging her husband's ministry.

Why is the pastor's wife the most important person in his life? The answer is quite simple: his ministry depends on it. If he neglects his wife, he may very well lose his ministry. Therefore, as a church, it is important that you encourage your pastor to care for and minister to his wife. You want your pastor's wife to be happy, and one of the key ways to assist her in this is to encourage her husband to meet her needs. As I mentioned in Chapter 5, there are ways you can encourage him in this. He could be encouraged to take time off and take a mini vacation or honeymoon with his wife annually. Encourage your pastor to take his wife out for a date regularly. Consider buying them a gift card to the theatre or a restaurant. Perhaps you could offer to babysit their children for an evening.

As a pastor, I have counselled many couples and instructed them to take time for themselves to build their relationship by establishing a date night once a week or taking a mini vacation at least once a year, but then I often ignored my very own advice and I regret that now. I have come to recognize how heeding this advice has strengthened my marriage and has built up my wife so that she is also better able to continue in ministry.

THE PASTOR'S WIFE MUST COME BEFORE THE CHURCH

One of the struggles the pastor often faces is the tension between cherishing his wife and serving the church family. There are many reasons to put the church family first. Sometimes it appears that his wife seems to have it all together and does not have needs that are as vital as that of the church family. I have to confess that I have struggled with this in the past. Although I am better at balancing it now, sometimes I still get it wrong.

In my early years as a pastor, I felt as though I was the only person who could meet the church family's needs. If someone called, I would run off to help him or her. This became my wife's frustration because our time was not cherished, which inevitably led to a struggle. As I mentioned in Chapter 1, I heard Dr. Joseph Stowell address this issue at a conference a number of year ago. He talked about how he would often run out on family events like birthdays and special dinners. He did this because someone called for help. Eventually, he learned to balance his time by asking some basic questions to determine whether the need was urgent. When I heard him speak, it was as though a light turned on in my head and I started to learn how to say "no". That is a hard word for a pastor to say, but it changed the way I do ministry.

At a different conference a few years later, I heard Dr. John Maxwell speak on the topic of the "super-pastor". He spoke about how a pastor can suffer from thinking that he can and should solve everyone's problems. Someone calls and he runs to the phone booth and flies over to be there. In reality, he gets into his car and drives over, all the while thinking that he is the solution to everyone's problems. In the meantime, his poor wife is left sitting at home feeling that everyone else is more important than she is. He knows that is not true, yet quite often that is the very message he conveys to her.

Who is at fault in this tug-of-war over the pastor's time and energy? First, it is the pastor's shortcoming. A pastor does not like to say, "No, not now." He actually may fear that the church will not like him or that his ministry to them will be hindered if he says no. Second, the church family is to bear some responsibility. Often the church family has unrealistic expectations of the pastor. Yes, we serve 24/7, but no one can actually serve that way for any significant amount of time without burning out or leaving.

In conclusion, it is important that your pastor set boundaries so that he can protect his most precious of all earthly relationships. That may mean that at times he will let people's expectations of him down. However, it also means that he will not let his wife down. In my experience, when I get this right, my wife has no problem with me caring for the church family, but when I get this wrong, ministry becomes a struggle.

HAPPY WIFE, HAPPY MINISTRY

We have all heard the saying, "Happy wife, happy life" or "If Mom is not happy, nobody is happy." This is true in ministry as well. Countless men have left either a particular ministry or the ministry altogether because their wives were not happy.

This is not to point a finger at the pastor's wife; this is to highlight the fact that a pastor's ministry is not somehow disconnected from the rest of his life. If his wife is not happy, that will affect his ministry. If a pastor neglects his first ministry, his ministry to his wife, then he may very well lose his latter ministry as well, his ministry to the church.

A pastor's wife could be unhappy for a number of

reasons. First, her unhappiness could be caused by her husband's neglect if he spends too much time away from her rather than building into her life. We have already looked at the importance of your pastor balancing this tug-of-war in his life. Second, her unhappiness could be caused by how people treat her within the church family or community.

I will cover how you can help your pastor's wife be happy in the next chapter in more detail, but worth mentioning here is the idea that you could be a friend to her.

THE PASTOR'S WIFE NEEDS HER HUSBAND

Because pastors move so frequently, the pastor's wife often does not have time to set down roots and become connected to the church family or the community. If she is shy and reserved, she needs her husband to assist her in the process of connecting.

The pastor is out several nights a week connecting with all kinds of people, but often his wife is at home with the children. She may find it hard to connect because of frequent moves, and sometimes because she has been hurt in this process. A pastor's wife can fear connecting so her husband becomes her lifeline. Sometimes a pastor's wife can become overwhelmed with all these new "friends" and may wonder if these folks would like her if she were not the pastor's wife.

The pastor's wife needs her husband for all of the normal reasons as well, including:

- Friendship
- Companionship
- Help around the house
- Someone to talk to
- Someone to pass the baton to after a stressful day with the kids
- Someone to unload on after the challenges of work

- Someone to just have fun with
- Someone who can give her his undivided attention

I encourage you to congratulate your pastor when he gets this right, and let him know how much you appreciate the fact the he takes good care of his wife. I cannot say this enough: board members need to strongly encourage their pastor to put his wife first, and not make him feel guilty for properly caring for his wife.

Chapter 7

THE PASTOR'S WIFE NEEDS GOOD RELATIONSHIPS IN THE CHURCH

THE LONELIEST PERSON IN THE CHURCH

Some wonder why the pastor's wife would be lonely; after all, look at all the people in the church that would love to be her friend! Frequently that is true; nevertheless, the pastor's wife seldom has close friends within the church for several reasons. Firstly, she may be put up on a pedestal where all admire her from a distance and treat her as if she is different from the other women in the church family. There are instances where she may even become the standard of dress and fashion in the church.

Secondly, everyone thinks everyone else is her friend so nobody reaches out to her thinking that someone else has already done so. In the meantime, she is left wondering whom to have as her friends. Take a moment to think about that. When was the last time you went out of your way to connect with your pastor's wife?

Thirdly, there may be politics involved, so she may feel that she has to be careful about not spending too much time with one person and not enough with another. It seems easier sometimes to just avoid the people altogether. She has probably been caught in political wars before and learned that she would rather not befriend women in the church.

Finally, sometimes she knows too much about what is going on behind the scenes causing her to want to withdraw and disconnect, especially if her husband or children have been hurt. Think about it this way: if someone at church or at work said something nasty about you or your spouse, would you be inclined to invite her over for a coffee? Probably not! For the pastor's wife, it can be very difficult to separate herself from the comments someone made at the annual business meeting about her husband, or the comment someone made about one of her children. Therefore, when that person shows up at church on Sunday all friendly and kind, she may not want to connect with them.

WHAT DOES A GOOD RELATIONSHIP LOOK LIKE?

There are several types of good relationships. A good working relationship involves people in the church and the pastor's wife working side by side without constantly feeling on guard lest they offend each other. Another good relationship can include disagreements without hurt feelings and trouble, where the pastor's wife can express her opinion without someone questioning, "That is the pastor's wife?" or "I wonder what the pastor thinks of that?"

The pastor's wife needs more than just good working relationships in the church. She also needs at least one good relationship with someone that is not her husband. She needs a woman she can talk to and be herself with. Someone with whom she can share her frustrations about the church and her husband. Someone with whom she can freely share without fear of judgement or something private getting out. She needs a confidant. However, this is not something that you or anyone can force, so do not go up to your pastor's wife and tell her that you are going to be her best friend, her confidant. There is a good chance that approach will not work.

What a woman can do, however, is make herself available. You can purposefully reach out to your pastor's wife. You and she may or may not become great friends, but one thing is for sure, she will know that someone is interested in her. This would most certainly help her with the loneliness.

In addition, you can try inviting a couple of women and your pastor's wife to coffee or lunch. Chances are a close friendship may develop from this sort of interaction. If, as a result, she develops a close relationship with someone other than you, choose not to get political about it or become offended. It would probably be best to thank the Lord that you assisted your pastor and his wife in this way.

WHY YOU WANT HER TO HAVE AT LEAST ONE GOOD RELATIONSHIP IN THE CHURCH

If no one reaches out to her, the pastor's wife may turn to someone else in or even beyond the community to find that relationship. However, a pastor's longevity may depend on the quality of his wife's relationships within the church. While the pastor may stay for the long haul despite his wife's relationships, the reality is that when the pastor's wife has no one in the church that she is close to, she will not feel tied to the church. When her husband gets discouraged, as he will, and starts to think about moving away, she will not be an advocate for the church. With no close relationships, she could just as easily move on.

Sometimes her loneliness becomes a point of conflict in the home, adding stress to the pastor's family life, which affects his ministry life as well. At a point when the ministry gets tough and your pastor wants to throw in the towel, it becomes easier to do so because leaving will help ease the conflict at home.

I strongly encourage you to honour your pastor's wife, not from a distance but personally. Let her know that you appreciate her, and do all you can to help her connect with the church family. Be sensitive to her personality. Not every pastor's wife is a people person, so maybe a small get together over coffee and dessert with a few of the women from the church would be more beneficial than inviting her to larger group activities. Ideally, inviting at least one woman in her age range would be beneficial. As well, do all you can to keep church politics out of your relationship. If she does not become your close friend, or even close to one or more of your close friends, choose to encourage her in whatever friendship she develops and choose not to hinder her from getting close to anyone in the church.

A word of caution and advice to the pastors' wives

reading this: as hard as it may feel at times, make every effort to connect with at least one woman in the church. Someone you can grow to trust or someone you can call on when you need a shoulder to cry on, other than your husband's shoulder. A good relationship is worth the risk in the end.

For those pastors' wives who have been hurt by such relationships, I encourage you to carefully seek out someone and slowly learn to trust again. It is still better to have someone you can learn to trust than to be lonely in ministry.

Chapter 8

The Pastor's Family Must Come First

THE PASTOR'S FAMILY MUST COME BEFORE THE CHURCH

Churches often struggle with double standards. On one hand, church members will think nothing of enrolling their children in organized sports or music classes. If their child's game is scheduled during a church event, there is no question as to where they will be – they will be at the game. On the other hand, if the pastor's child is in the same game, where does everyone expect the pastor to be? At the church because that is his job. He cannot take that time off to go watch his child play a game. Here we have the double standard. There is one for the parishioner's family and one for the pastor and his family.

I have been blessed in my ministry life. I have been able to attend almost all the events in which my children have been involved. If it were during the day, I would organize my schedule so that I could be there. The times that I found most challenging to schedule were around Wednesday night Bible study and prayer meeting as well as Sunday programs. As a pastor, I should be at the Bible study, or at church, yet as a father, I should be at my child's event. I must say that I did not always get this right. Most times, I attended the Bible study or church service instead of my child's event. Some will criticize me for this statement, but as a Christian father, my first ministry should be my family.

The first year I coached my daughter's fastball team, I specifically asked that they not schedule our team for any Wednesday evening games. Of course, that summer we had a game every Wednesday. There was a choice to make. As a coach, should I miss every Wednesday game, showing the pagan world that I was a good Christian who attended Bible study? As a father, should I put work first, showing my daughter that the church was more important than she was?

As a pastor, should I put my daughter's needs ahead of those of the church? Could there be a way to compromise without stepping away from God's calling in relation to the community, my daughter, and the church?

In the end, we scheduled the Bible study for Thursday evenings that summer, which worked out well until tournament time. With a game scheduled during the Sunday morning service, I faced another big decision. I scheduled a guest speaker for that Sunday, and I was available to coach the team. Consequently, people in the church saw that I valued my daughter, and it spoke volumes to them. I coached for three years, and to this day, girls still ask me if I would coach again, and no one in the church even remembers that I rescheduled the Wednesday night Bible study.

Encourage your pastor to put his family first. Obviously, he cannot be at the hockey arena every Sunday morning, but maybe he could for the occasional tournament. This will help your pastors' relationship with his children, and in turn help him in his ministry as well. Some of his children's well-being may be attributed to the fact that they know Dad loves them and will put them first before the ministry. As a result, your pastor will have more freedom to do the ministry without feelings of resentment toward the church family.

WHAT DOES IT PROFIT A PASTOR TO...LOSE HIS KIDS?

Sometimes pastors focus so much on Kingdom building that they lose sight of the most important people in their lives. Next to their spouses, that should be their children.

At my first church where I was senior pastor, an older gentleman gave me some sobering advice that helped me with my natural tendency toward overworking. His advice was, "Pace yourself, because when you are gone no one will remember all the hard work you did." He was not saying do not work hard, as he himself was a hard worker. What he meant was to keep perspective. Pastors sometimes think that they are going to change the world, and in so doing they lose the very world they could have changed – their children's.

Years ago, before I was married and had children, I heard a sermon that influenced my life. The sermon helped form my view of the importance of keeping a balance between my ministry and my family. The sermon was entitled "What does it profit a pastor to win the whole world for God and lose his own kids?" The point was clear: do not sacrifice your family on the altar of ministry. God does not promise to take care of your pastor's personal business if your pastor puts the church first. This would be like saying that God will take care of your family if you put your career first. We would all say if someone puts their career first, they would risk losing their children. May I challenge you to encourage your pastor to put quality time and energy into his family? This is necessary so that he might not lose his children.

It is very unfortunate that many corporations want their employees to put the company first. This has caused some people to lose their families. The question I would like you to contemplate is this: should the church be the kind of place that would be willing to sacrifice their pastor's family for the sake of church growth? What is the stronger testimony: that of a pastor who built a mega church, planted dozens of churches, but lost his children to the world, or the pastor whose children love and serve the Lord and appreciate their parent's ministry?

HELP YOUR PASTOR PUT HIS FAMILY FIRST

As previously mentioned in Chapter 5, encourage your pastor to take time off and do not let him get away with working 24/7. If you are a board member, hold him accountable to taking time off. If you know that his child is in a special event, encourage him to make that event a priority, and help him with any details like pulpit supply or leading the mid-week service. If you can encourage your pastor in this way, he will last a lot longer in your church. He will have the support that he needs to care for and minister to his family.

Pastors, if you struggle in this area, allow your board or a special friend to hold you accountable. Let them assist you in this area of life. Your wife and family will thank you for it and in the end, you will be glad you did.

Chapter 9

THE PASTOR'S KIDS ARE JUST KIDS

THAT IS THE PASTOR'S KID

My wife and I have done all we can to keep the fact that our children are pastor's kids a secret from them. We thought we had done a good job of keeping this secret, but our now adult children informed us that it was pointed out to them and to others about them, quite frequently.

We chose not to expect anything more from our children than we would expect from any other child in the church. Nonetheless, the church held a higher standard for our children than they held for their own. Please remember, your pastor's kids are just kids. Some children can sit still, some cannot. Some obey and are fully compliant, while others are not. Choose not to hold your pastor's children to a higher standard than your own. If you do not have children, use the standard you would expect of any other child in the church.

Here are some questions to consider:

- Why would people point out the pastor's kids to newcomers?
- Why would newcomers need to know who the pastor's kids are?
- What message does this attention send to the pastor's kids?

People seem to feel the need to make sure everyone knows who these special children are; however, this kind of attention does not make them feel special, it makes them feel spotlighted and self-conscious. According to *Life-Line for Pastors*, "Eighty percent of adult children of pastors surveyed have had to seek professional help for depression...These statistics came from across denominational lines, and have been garnered from various reliable sources such as Pastor to Pastor, Focus on the Family, Ministries Today, Charisma Magazine, TNT Ministries, Campus Crusade for Christ and the Global Pastors Network." [3] If eighty percent of pastor's children have had to seek professional help for depression, obviously this data suggests that holding them to a higher standard than other children in the church is taking a toll on them.

MANY PARENTS OR CHILDREN OF THE CHURCH

Imagine yourself at your grandparents' for Christmas along with all your aunts and uncles. Everyone will be together for a week. Can you feel the excitement, the chaos, the confusion, and the potential for conflict? Grandma tells you to play with your toys downstairs, while Aunt Cranky orders you to get up stairs. Uncle No-Fun instructs you to get outside, while Cousin Exasperated complains, "Don't play here, go to the other side of the yard and play ball there." Frustrated, you just lose it and start to whip the ball at the front door because no one else knows that your mother and father already gave you the ground rules before you ever got there. They told you to not upset Aunt Cranky and to stay out of the way of Cousin Exasperated. Under too much pressure with everyone acting like your parent and not knowing who to listen to, you become confused and frustrated and just choose not to listen to anyone.

Now transfer the scenario to the church and the pastor's kid and multiply it by fifty-two weeks a year. Mrs. Cranky and Mr. Exasperated are there every time the pastor's child does something they should not and rather than simply pointing out the misbehavior, they claim parental status and correct the child. The pastor's children do not have just one

---

[3] Murphy, R. A. (2002). Statistics about Pastors. *Maranatha Life's Life-Line for Pastors*. Retrieved from http://www.MaranathaLife.com

Mom and Dad watching over them, but many Moms and Dads. Often these adults offer conflicting messages and instructions. Is there any wonder why the pastor's children often rebel and walk away from the church.

DO NOT RUIN YOUR DAD'S MINISTRY

Unintentionally, children are bound to make liars out of their parents and embarrass them. This fact can become problematic for pastor's kids because of church members' high expectations and the potential reality that they will judge the pastor harshly. Some church members will use his children's behavior against him, sometimes in a malicious manner.

I have often heard someone say, "The pastor was nice, but his kids were a problem." This environment adds so much unfair and unnecessary stress to a child's life. Consider this situation in terms of a family breakup. Is it ever acceptable to blame the kids? Everyone would of course say no. However, as soon as you allow this attitude in the church family, you allow the child's behavior to dictate the future of your relationship with your pastor.

As mentioned in Chapter 4, often the pastor's children's behaviour is used against him. The criticism is that if the pastor cannot manage his children, then he should not be a pastor. People will even quote Scripture to prove their point. I need to restate the fact that these people have misused the Scriptures or forgotten two things. First, when a child misbehaved in Biblical times, the father could do with his child as he wished; there was no excuse for disrespectful children. Second, in Biblical times there were no teenagers. You were either a child under your parents' control or an adult. As adults, they were no longer under their parents' control but married off. I will be covering this topic extensively in my second book entitled, *Biblical Grounds for Dismissing Your Pastor*.

What effect does this type of criticism have on your

pastor's children and your pastor? It causes destruction because the pastor's kids feel like pawns in a battle between the church and their father, the pastor. Similar to parents who play the kids off between each other in a divorce, this kind of criticism only serves to harm the kids. Furthermore, it hurts your pastor. There are times that as a parent, through no fault of your own, you lose your kids. To have someone rub that in your face does not help. Most parents who have a wayward child already feel that they are losers, so using the situation as ammunition against them is not an astute thing to do. What your pastor needs is for you to come alongside him and encourage him. Turning on him in his challenging time of dealing with a wayward child is utterly dreadful. It can cause your pastor to become disillusioned, lose heart, and often becomes the catalyst that ends the pastor's ministry in a particular church, and often all together.

Chapter 10

CLOSING REMINDERS

THREE THINGS THAT WILL HINDER YOUR PASTOR

First, do not foster a critical spirit. It is easy to be critical because it does not require a brain, just a mouth; helping develop solutions takes brains. Some people feel that they are God's gift to their pastor to keep him humble. However, people with this attitude can cause their pastor to experience the "toonie effect" that I described in Chapter 4. If you think your role in the church is to keep your pastor humble, consider Jesus' words in Luke 22:22: "For indeed, the Son of Man is going as it has been determined; but woe to that man by whom He is betrayed!" I will venture as far as to say that this principle can be applied to your relationship with your pastor: you do not want to be the person who causes him grief. As Hebrews 13:17 instructs, let him lead you with joy, not grief.

Second, guard against an unteachable heart. Knowing there are people in the congregation who are so set in their ways that they cannot learn is disheartening for your pastor. At times, I have explained a black and white concept that needs no interpretation directly from the Bible, and the unteachable heart still refuses to accept it. For example, according to Luke 2:39-40, after Jesus was born in Bethlehem, and after the shepherds had come and gone, but well before the wise men arrived, Mary and Joseph took the baby Jesus to Jerusalem, then returned home to Nazareth. This means that sometime after that, but still before the wise men arrived, they moved back to Bethlehem and lived in a house. Yet, even after examining the text, I know of people who persist in believing that Jesus was in Bethlehem until the wise men showed up, and then moved to Egypt and eventually to Nazareth. The point is, be teachable.

Third, do not impose a demanding regime upon your

pastor. No one can work 24/7, not even 16/6. It will eventually kill them: physically, emotionally and most importantly, spiritually. I am not advocating that pastors should have an easy life. I know from experience that if your pastor loves God and God's people that he will work harder than he should. It is foolish, however, to demand that your pastor be in the office from nine to five, as well as be out several evenings a week and on weekends. The idea should not be to squeeze as much out of him as we can for as long as he is here, but instead to help him serve here for as long as we can.

THREE THINGS THAT WILL HELP YOUR PASTOR

First, pray for your pastor and let him know that you are praying for him. Follow Paul's example as in Colossians 1:9 when he reminds the Colossians that he is praying for them. It is vital that you encourage your pastor by letting him know that you are holding him up in prayer. You could even ask him if there is anything you could pray for on his behalf.

Second, do all you can to be an encourager, not a discourager. Every pastor I know has more than enough discouragers, but never too many encouragers. Never fear overdoing encouragement. Send him a note, take him out for coffee, and show him that you understood the message on Sunday. The standard, "Good sermon today, Pastor" is as empowering as the comments made during the receiving line at a wedding with 300 or more guests, so try to say something more meaningful. Also, remember that at the door after the sermon is not the time to correct your pastor's sermon, but to encourage your pastor. Finally, give your pastor a night out with his wife, or a weekend away, and babysit the children or help make arrangements to have them watched. Use your imagination! If you would appreciate something that someone could do for you, chances are, so would your pastor. And if you are not sure, just ask.

Third, assist your pastor in ministering to his wife and family. Do not call on your pastor's day off unless someone has passed away. Recognize and protect your pastor's time with his family. Understand that it is a very good thing for your pastor to spend time with his family, so encourage him to attend his children's special events at school and in the community, even if that means rescheduling a church program or providing someone to fill in for him. Consider if the church needs to add staff so as not to over burden your pastor. That staff could be a paid position or a volunteer. Many pastors work nearly seventy hours a week, which may be fine for a short stint, but over the long haul affects every aspect of his ministry and may even end his ministry for your church and in some cases all together.

Chapter 11

For Pastors Only

STUDY AND PRAY

I know that most of us do not need to be told to study, but to pray – that may be different. This is not meant to be a lecture, but as a pastor myself, I know that I love to study, but prayer is often more challenging. May I encourage you in both, be in the Word, study hard, and enjoy it much. And then take time to pray. You should learn to pray and to love it. Depending on the size of your congregation, pray for every family every week. I liked going down the pews and standing where people regularly sat and praying for them right there. I found that it kept me awake and focused on the people God entrusted to me. When the church gets too large for that, there are still ways to uphold them in prayer. If you have staff, pray together. I find that those times of praying together are the best. We do this almost every day and it strengthens our bond.

EXERCISE IS GOOD FOR THE BODY AND THE SOUL

Exercise is not a bad or evil thing that should be avoided at all costs. In 1 Timothy 4:8, Paul describes exercise as "of little good," not of "no good". We would be wise to remember that Paul walked everywhere; if we were able to do that, we might not need the gym either. However, since we drive most places and then sit, eat and drink coffee or tea with more treats than we need, we may find that although it has no eternal value per say, exercise may prolong our ministry usefulness and a lack thereof may cut our ministry life short.

YOUR SPOUSE IS PRIORITY NUMBER ONE

This was a lesson I had to learn and God used my wife to help me learn. I had been raised by a pastor father who defiantly put ministry first. He loved my mom and us kids, but the church came first. So this was a difficult lesson for me. I thank God that I am learning this. I do not always get it right, but my wife is good at reminding me. For longevity in my ministry, it was so important for me to learn this.

DO NOT LOSE YOUR KIDS

God has not promised to raise your kids if you lay them on the altar of ministry. Many pastors' kids end up in trouble because of the high expectations of everyone around them and the low involvement of their father, the pastor, who is out saving the world. As pastors, we sometimes think that we are going to change the world, and in so doing we lose the very world we could have changed, the world of our children. Let's be careful not to fall into that trap.

DEVELOP OTHER LEADERS WHO CAN TAKE OVER

I have found that many pastors feel threatened by the younger guys coming up behind them and that concerns me. I love the young men on my staff. They are not a threat, they are my best assets. They will lead the church well beyond where I might. I welcome the new ideas they have, and we have already planed that one of them will replace me. We have also allowed the men of our church to practice preaching. Several young men have attended Bible College as a direct result of preaching and realizing that this is what God would have them do for life.

BE WATCHFUL FOR BURNOUT

Take time to rest. Recently I attended a workshop on "The Forgotten Spiritual Discipline of R&R." I discovered that God never tells us to worship on the Sabbath, but that we are only told to rest. What is rest? Ultimately it is doing something that causes you to relax and unwind. It does not have to be time in the Word, though it can be. It could be a game of golf or fishing. For some like myself, it could even be cutting the grass; it has a beginning and an end. Because our "job" is never-ending we can so easily just keep working but if we do not rest, it will catch up with us.

DEVELOP GOOD FRIENDS

As a pastor, it is important to have good friends. Look for people with whom you can socialize that are not your peers, not your ministry. They can be from your congregation, but should be people who minister to you as much, if not more, than you do to them. You need a friend with whom you can laugh, cry, or just be your non-pastor self.

SHARPEN YOUR SKILLS

I have been pastoring for well over twenty-seven years and I am still learning new things. Recently, I learned how to preach from an iPad. I am also learning to preach from my iPhone at some point in the near future. These skills are relatively easy, but we also need to learn new skills to take the church family to the next level.

As a pastor, I do not want to be like the mom I described who decided to move on to a new family because she had never raised teenagers before. I want to be the caregiver who finds some good books on teenagers or talks to someone who has teenagers to develop the skills to deal with them. As pastors, we need to recognize that we need further education even if we are not going for our doctorate. Can we be honest with ourselves? At times, we feel that we need to move on because we do not have the skills to serve the church we have been charged with at this time. Stop. Rather than moving on, perhaps all we require is to retool.

THE ADULT CHILD OF A DYSFUNCTIONAL CHURCH

I will attempt to write a book on this subject in the future, but I wanted to note here the idea that often, a pastor's greatest struggle is with the "power people" or those individuals who have been in the church for a long time. They have seen pastors come and go and watched as the church grew more and more dysfunctional. In a physical family where the primary caregiver has come and gone, often one of the children takes on the caregiver role. I would like to propose that the power people we struggle with are like the children of a dysfunctional family; they have become the primary caregivers of the church. Instead of fighting them for power, we need to find a loving and compassionate way to give them permission to release that responsibility. This progress will only happen if pastors are able and willing to stay for the long haul.

Manufactured by Amazon.ca
Bolton, ON